EXPOSE' OF THE HEART

By:

Nita L. Chase

EXPOSE' OF THE HEART

Nita L. Chase

PHENOMENAL
Jas ENTERPRISE

ISBN: 978-1-7356265-4-3 (Paperback)

ISBN: 978-1-7356265-5-0 (Ebook - EPUB)

Library of Congress Control Number: 2020925727

Cover Design by Arash Jahani
Book Format by Arash Jahani
Art Credits: TheRudyKing - Page 107 and
Nenyatta Smith - Page 13.

Printed in the United States of America. First Printing
Edition 2021.

PhenomenalJas Enterprise LLC

13815 Ginger Lane

Gulfport, Mississippi, 39503

www.phenomenaljasenterprise.com

DEDICATED TO MY SIBLINGS

Bonnie,

Blazing as elder in the sisterhood

Ordering life to obey her command

Never ending is her cycle of giving

Notably remembering her heritage of love

Institutionalizing the foundation of greatness

Eternally igniting the home fires of family

Gwendolyn,

Generosity exposed fully at her expiration

Winner recognized at her demise

Exhaling but never finding release

Nipping at the elixir of life

Dazed by interruptions in her score

Obstinate in her chosen stance

Loving those in the forgotten realm

Yearning for unconditional invitation to be

Nostalgically seeking the time before darkness

Lavonne,

Looking forward to the clear future

Aftermath no longer in tow

Victoriously standing on the mountains climbed

Over debt that kept her bound

Noticing today the hidden of yesterday

Naked before the living God

Evolving daily towards final destination

Ladwaina,

Laughing despite borderline state of affairs

Agonizing over another's misfortune

Draining herself to harvest her seeds

Walking a tight rope balanced by hope

Acknowledging the Word; lives and gives

Imagining a future on showcase tomorrow

Nurturing dreams into manifestations

Abounding to face another day

Edna,

Evolving from youthful desires and delights

Daring enemies to enter her domain

Negating obstacles that cross her highway

Abounding before her feet hit the ground

Ricky,

Reticent by nature

Instrumental by situation dictation

Concerned even in silence

Keen when blindfold lifted or when least expected

Yielding to God Almighty

Thank you for all of it

ACKNOWLEDGEMENTS

To my A's who shouted and whispered Amens
To my B's who Barricaded me from nay-sayers
To my C's Charismatics who seasoned poetic escapes
To my D's Discerners and Distractors who kept my toes on point
To my E's who Echoed in my silence
To my F's, Fanatic's, whose accolades still crescendos
To my H's who Historically are parts of this journey
To my I's who encouraged my I can do
To my J's who led me to word Juxtapositions
To my K's who Kept step to my timeline
To my L's who Lusciously kissed my vocabulary
To my M's, Martyrs who submitted to word slaughter
To my N's who Nostalgically refused to retreat
To my O's, Offender's, who gave me haters to pen
To my P's, Partyer's who shared an elixir or two
To my Q's, Quill's that forward pressed my pen
To my R's, Reenters, who became poetic resources
To my S's who Sermon-aided a little word foreplay
To my T's, Testimonial's, who helped fuel my faith
To my U's, Upper's who challenged me to up my ante
To my V's, Villains who antagonized my uncensored lips
To my W's, Worshipper's who prostrated before God with me
To my X's, X-Rayers who edited with the light of God
To my Y's, Yoke's that could not harness my gift

To my Z's, Zealots who always followed my fire

I Shout

THANK YOU ALL

Contents

Chapter 5

YES, I AM MY SISTER'S KEEP-HER —   106

ABOUT THE AUTHOR —   134

FOREWORD

For centuries women have stood as the backbone of public powerful men, yet, far too often, fail to bolster the courage to publicly present themselves authentically to the world. Instead, women often play a plethora of roles resulting in an unfortunate identity crisis.

Expose' of the Heart is a collection of poetry that provokes the reader to explore and discover the internal self. In a positive manner, it lays bare expressions of forgiveness, alienation, and self-love in the setting of real-life experiences. It offers often unspoken words to encourage bravery throughout the feminine journey; one that welcomes a unique encounter between intimacy and love. Each poetic piece paints an electrifying picture of a woman's engagement with pain, passion, and power.

Throughout this work, Nita introduces the necessity of self: adapting a healthy self-concept, while traveling the road of self-discovery, and ultimately obtaining self-fulfillment. Her eccentric writing style challenges readers to boldly search within and embrace their internal, God-given, value. It is the insight into the depths of the intrinsic search that leads to a truth which enables confrontation with unseen fears, emotional ambiguity, and misgivings. Nita's dynamic expressions beautifully encapsulate organic life moments from her personal journey which will undoubtedly echo many of the experiences of her reading audience.

Expose' of the Heart seeks to encourage women seeking freedom and self-expression during this unprecedented cultural juncture for women in 2020. The dichotomy of this current period in history is indeed of great nuance. While there remain women in parts of the world who are oppressed, stripped of basic human rights, and expected to be seen rather than heard; we are also living in a time where women are the Heads of States and governmental decision making. The poetic concepts throughout Expose' of the Heart speaks to the full spectrum of female stories that creatively encourage all women to self-emerge and unapologetically embrace their true being.

Thank you, Nita, for this imperative collection of art that masterfully reflects self-appreciation and connectivity with inner-self and others. May all humanity embrace its essences as a playground for passion and develop the courage to play loud and free. Within its creative motif, may Expose' of the Heart avert alienation and foster life-giving relationships between self, others, and God. I pray each reader connects with and finds new ways to express their stories from the pages of this remarkable collection.

Shirley Brown, R.N.
Health and Life Coach
Ocean Springs, Mississippi

C h a p t e r   1

4 PLAY

Moan

A + 40

My Richard Loves My Kitty

Give Me Forever Romance

Every Moment In Between

I Got Caught Up

Oh What A Night To Remember

Make Me Again

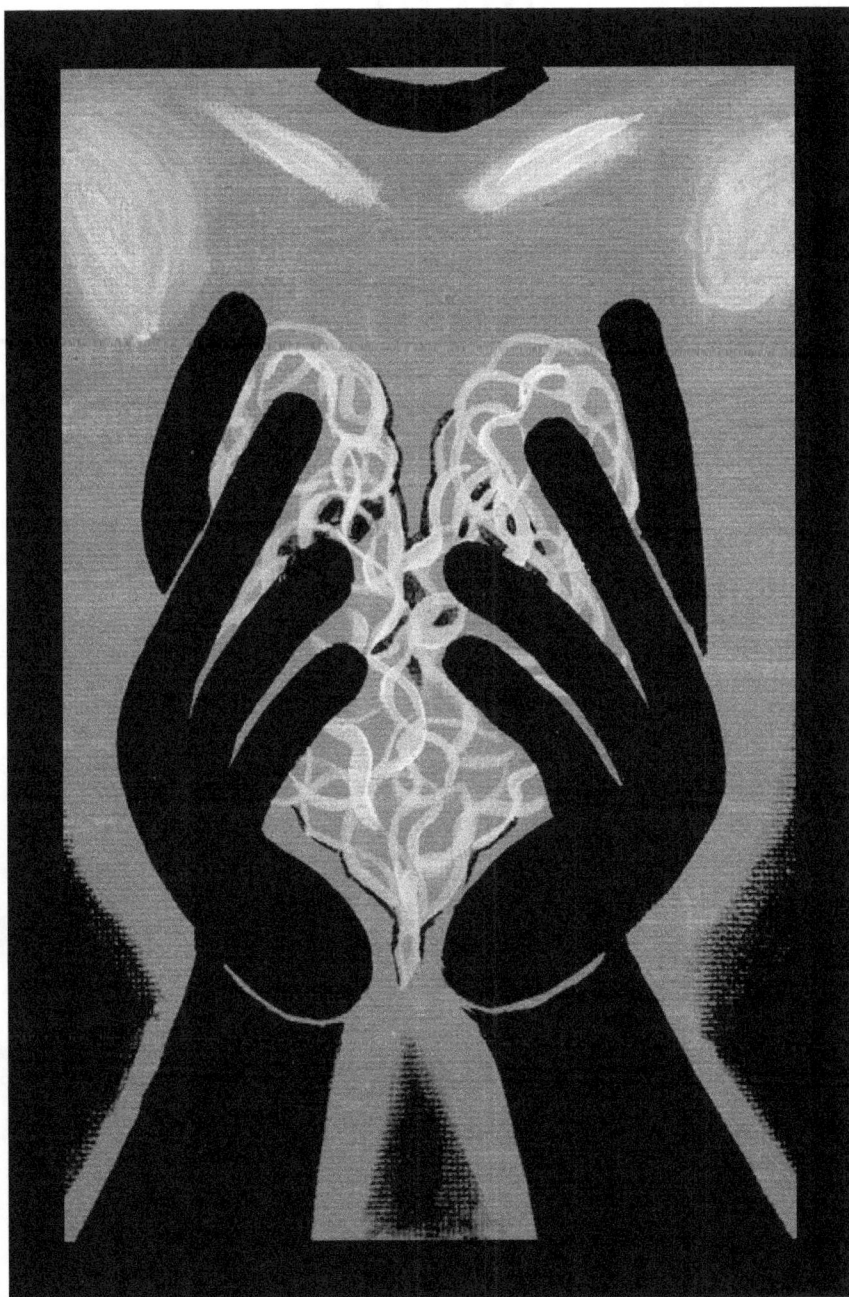

MOAN

MOAN

M

O

A

N

Mmm Mer Mercy

Mercy

is in my moan

seducing a mercenary to locate my depth of despair

and restore the core of my joy

to heights of ecstasy

MOAN

M

O

A

N

M O Oh Oh OHHHHHH Opportunity

is in the midst of my of my moan

And when recognized

it is transformed into

the knock knock that is answered

MOAN

M

O

A

N

M O A A Attitude

is in my moan

determining the strength of the climax

and the timetable

of conclusion

MOAN

M

O

A

N

M O A N N Nos

Nostalgia
is in my moan

Napping

Nesting

Nipping

Noting

Nudging

Me

to moan

One

More

Time

© *Nita L. Chase 2005*

A + 40

40 is the end of testing

and baby you receive an A+ on many examinations

First, I tested your eyes

and you passed the sparkle test

For today the windows of your soul

are still brilliantly shining

to guide me to your heart

And the sun and moon of life did not dim the vision

A+

Although your eyes led me to your heart

your smile passed the second test

And today, like yesterday

I melt as ice cream before the sun

every time your lips

display the sign of pure joy

A+

Thirdly, I tested your ears

not the shape

but their understanding of my silent echoes

and whispers in the cave of my dark hours

while you calmly soothed me with lyrics of love

until our passion became soulful musicality

A+

You scored genius level on test four

as your touch has broken world records in my book

Just thinking of the warmth in your every embrace

causes an eruption from my center core

Your skillful fingers played my body like a Steinway

and the music of our first-born seed was birthed

A+

At test five you reached the pinnacle

and I no longer test you

I favor you

For you are

A

+

all the Godly things TBA (to be addressed)

© Nita L. Chase 2009

MY RICHARD LOVES MY KITTY

My Richard loves my Kitty

So I keep her free from litter

ensures she's sweet, never tart never bitter

For Richard loves to stroke her

so he can hear her softly purr

My Richard loves my Kitty

For he smiles every time he sees her arch

And from attn hut he begins to march

He never wants to leave her side

He often takes her for a ride

and sometimes Richard lets her drive

My Richard loves my Kitty

He wakes her often from her nap

to spend some time on his lap

And Richard softly calls her "pussy cat"

and thinks OMG this cat is phat

My Richard loves my Kitty

So I keep her safe from dogs
and all the other nuts on logs
For Kitty's aim is to please
my Richard who loves her indeed
and Kitty does it with such ease

My Richard loves my Kitty

I told you so

Now you know

blow by blow

© *Nita L. Chase 2010*

GIVE ME FOREVER ROMANCE

Give me forever romance

that each time we seal our lips

we unlock a sumptuous

paradise of sensuality

Give me forever romance

that the simple brush of your fingertips

paints a rainbow of delight in my heart

as it beats to your rhythmic flow

Give me forever romance

The kind that causes an inferno

that ignites with each flicker

of your flaming torch of love

Give me forever romance

And forever

claim the passion of dance

in our romance

perpetually

© Nita L. Chase 2010

EVERY MOMENT IN BETWEEN

Every moment in between your kiss

I miss

Every moment in between the touch of your hand

the next touch I plan

Every moment in between your smile

is just the longest mile

Every moment in between your smell

I spend time in jail

Every moment away from your eyes

my heart aches and cries

Every moment in between your thrust

I don't trust

Every moment you leave my side

that moment feels too wide

Every moment you don't whisper in my ear

other sounds I refuse to hear

Every moment in between your sensual moan

I groan

Every moment in between the brush of your fingertip

I need to get a grip

Every moment in between sleeping next to you

I don't have a clue

Every moment in between your arms not encircling me

is not the place to be

Every moment in between you and me

is an eternity

I don't need

© Nita L. Chase 2010

I GOT CAUGHT UP

I got caught up

It began with my butterfly kisses across your lips

but I got caught up

and the flutter retreated to allow my tongue

to engage yours in a dance

I got caught up

I got caught up

I started out by brushing your hand

but I got caught up

And began to stroke your canvas

until an explosion of colors erupted

I got caught up

I got caught up

I started embracing you for the moment

but I got caught up

and my arms refused to let go

of your stature

until I traveled to the ecstasy point

I got caught up

I got caught up

Caught up in your two lips

Caught up in your applauding hands

Caught up in your safety blanket arms

Caught up in all

in between

your head, heart, and heels

And until you loose me

I

am

trapped

© *Nita L. Chase. August 26, 2012*

OH WHAT A NIGHT TO REMEMBER

Oh what a night

You see every facet was just right

The moonlight remembers it oh too well

For it bathed us in its perfect light

and witnessed things we dare not tell

Oh What A Night

You know the splendor in the grass kind

Where the crickets chirp to your beat

and you're drunk from love not from wine

and passion surpasses a volcano's heat

Oh what a night

Mr. Owl blinked as it stared in awe

The night blooming jasmine perfumed the air

We did things which may have been against the law

and made one-of-a-kind works of art extremely rare

Oh this was a memorable night

You whispered love notes to make me sing your song
The creatures of the shadows stayed out of sight
This was the night we could do no wrong
So I'll repeat it even in the sunlight

Oh what a night

Oh what a night

Oh what a night

Right?

© Nita L. Chase 2010

MAKE ME AGAIN

Make me again

Make me say that again
You know the that
that I first whispered
when we began lips
and fingertips foreplay
under the moon

Make me again

Make me touch you there again
You know the secret spot
that only true love discovered
as we blanketed each other
in naked truth
skin to skin

Make me again

Make me do that thing again
You know the thing that I did

when you did

what you did

to make me do the do

that I did

when you did

what you did

in our secret boudoir

Make me again

Make me scream your name again

You know the name that I screamed

when I declared to heaven a praise report

about the way you thrill

and make me feel sensations

God bestowed

in the Garden of Eden

Make me again

Make me sing that song again

You know the song I sing

from the pinnacle of ecstasy

induced by every facet of your

intoxicating lovemaking

Make me again

And again

And again

© *Nita L. Chase June 6, 2008*

C h a p t e r 2

THE G SPOT

Get God Out

Scarlett Letter # 33

God of Healing and Inspiration

Heaven's Court

In the Secret Place

It's Not about Me

Somebody's Got to Pay the Price

Before and After OMG
(Oh My God)

GET GOD OUT

So you want me to get God out

OK I will, just listen to me shout

Get God Out

Out into my sister's workplace

so her boss will see God all over her face

Get God Out

Out into my brother's home

that his feet will not to and fro roam

Get God Out

Out and on board the luxury cruise ship

to keep another ocean liner from taking a dip

and to be the wine the cruisers sip

Get God Out

Out into the mean streets and down memory lane

so our nation can stop raising so much cain

Get God Out

Out among the gang bangers and gun strappers

worldly rappers and bootie tappers

See them change into Godly praise flappers

Get God Out

Out into the shelter for the homeless

to give them shelter and success

Get God Out

Out into that one's prison cell

to unloose the chains and sound the liberty bell

Get God Out

Out into the schools of miseducation

to solve the crisis and frustration

Get God Out

Out into every hospital room
to erase the doom and winter of gloom

Get God Out

Out into the drug infested allies
Watch addicts lead praise rallies

Get God Out

Out into each denomination
and into every proclamation
until "In God I am"
is a unified declaration

Get God Out

So you want me to get God out

So you want me to get God out

Watch Me

© *Nita L. Chase 2010*

SCARLETT LETTER # 33

I still read Scarlett Letter # 33

A love letter written to me

Line by line I am yet amazed

by the passion in the word

My mind is blown and dazed

by the oratory I heard

Line by line I am yet amazed

by the passion on each page

My mind is blown and dazed

Truly this can't be duplicated on stage

This letter reads

like music to my ear

And to every heart

that is eager to hear

Each line is sealed

with my lover's kiss

Reading his love letter

is pure bliss

His love letter is

a scarlet sealed decree

that he finalized

at age thirty-three

He wrote me this letter

that I may live

His sweat, blood

and very life He did give

Scarlett Letter #33

was posted on a tree

for me

that I may be free

This treasured letter

was then buried in the ground

A more precious gem

will never be found

I will always read Scarlett Letter #33

to ensure I maintain my identity

© Nita L. Chase 2012

GOD OF HEALING AND INSPIRATION

God heals me

You may thrill me momentarily on Blueberry Hill

temporarily rock my world with zest and zeal

touch my one spot that was dormant afore you

make my pulse dance to counts and do what it do

But be not mistaken

God heals me

Past Blueberry Hill

beyond your time sensitive thrill

with immeasurable zest

and He never takes a rest

God heals me

From head to toe

His anointing makes me glow

propels me to stratospheres like never before

I'll worship Him forever more

God heals me

God inspires me

Your motivational speech captures me for the hour

For that 60-minute time span I feel I have the power

By the words you exhale my heart begins to thump

In that time space I feel eager to leap and jump

But be not misinformed

God inspires me

He orates and I am transformed

Priestly and kingly garments I begin to adorn

The joy of His word dictates my duration

and becomes the path to my final destination

God inspires me

When He speaks, I am mesmerized

by His whispers that crescendos and tantalize

Then possibilities obey my every command

as I march victoriously across the land

God heals and inspires

with a passion unequaled

that requires no sequel

For God heals and inspires

to

perfection

© *Nita L. Chase 2012*

HEAVEN'S COURT

You talk about things

done in my past

How I was once

considered low class

You gossip about things

I used to do

who I did it with

and who I did it to

But I now tell you

this undisputed fact

no speculation

nor part of an act

no mystery

nor old folk tale

I'm not guilty

and won't go to hell

Fact!

My trial will be held

in heaven's court on high

I'll be found not guilty

and I tell you why

When my accusers stand

before my Father's throne

My DNA (Divinely Nobly Acquitted) exonerates me

from all wrong

For in heaven's court

my Father is my judge

Against His own

He holds no grudge

The verdict He gives

is mercy and grace

sealed by Jesus

who never lost a case

Fact...

© *Nita L. Chase 2012*

IN THE SECRET PLACE

In the secret place

I find paradise

I'm hidden from their eyes

Hidden from their lies

in the secret place

In the secret place

I hear your love song

You never hit a note wrong

Make me feel right at home

in the secret place

In the secret place

I find a special peace

My mind is at ease

We do a little strip tease

in the secret place

In the secret place

I taste and see mercy

Your grace never leaves me

We bask in ecstasy

in the secret place

And this is one secret

I refuse to keep

© Nita L. Chase 2012

IT'S NOT ABOUT ME

It's not about me

It's about He

He that talks and walks the same

and knows my every game

It's not about me

It's about He

He who lives

and every day gives

He who is truth, life, and way

Again I say

It's not about me

It's about He

He who always hears

and stills my fears

It's not about me

She

They

Us

For despite us

God is still just

And know this my friend

it will forever be

Not about us

But eternally about

He

© *Nita L. Chase 2012*

SOMEBODY'S GOT TO PAY THE PRICE

Half truths and little white lies

have become great big sin colored tales

told by the young and old alike

And guess what

Somebody's got to pay the price

Too little too late

once a phrase for missed opportunities

is more and more a reality show

in the minds of too many

And guess what

Somebody's got to pay the price

By any means necessary

in the yesteryears

was declared with a master plan

But now it is ever present

without forethought or regret

And guess what

Somebody's got to pay the price

E quality and jus...tice

are sometimes mirages

on America's constitution

that the Supreme Court

highlights with decision

And guess what

Somebody's got to pay the price

In God we trust

used to be engraved

in the heart of America

Yet as we pass the middle

evolve towards the end

God becomes a faded memory

of who our forefathers said they knew

And guess what

Somebody's got to pay the price

Somebody's got to pay

for the lies
in disguise

for waking up too late
dismissing love in pursuit of hate

for living on the devil's stage
as though God feels no hurt or rage

for never achieving heaven on earth
nor knowing the extent of your worth

Somebody's got to pay

And somebody will pay

Someday

© Nita L. Chase 2012

BEFORE AND AFTER OMG (OH MY GOD)

Before OMG

My seconds were like hours

My hours were like years

with Niagara Falls saturation

of unquenchable tears

Before OMG

I had a heart of desperation

lacking self identification

longing for justification

worth dictated by a man's oration

Before OMG

Hungry and homeless

thirsty and oppressed

midnight on every street

wallowing in defeat

Before OMG

Broken and torn

from the wrath of his scorn

Vulnerability made it easy

for my enemies to seize me

For every before there is an after

After OMG

Minute by minute I am filled with joy

The armor of God I now deploy

For I am protected from mass destruction

No longer a pawn for the devil's abduction

After OMG

The shield of God's grace has covered me

erasing pain and rejection from my memory

I'm allowing love to flood the barriers of my heart

breaking the chains that kept us apart

After OMG

In my life God now reigns supreme

and no, it's not always peaches and crème

But with the bitter, tart, and the sour

God gives me peace hour by hour as He is my tower

After OMG

May my life become the precedent

for those who are still hellbent

And may the light of God in me be seen

as I walk boldly in service to the King

The befores of my past

God overpowered at last

and now I am free

to shout

OMG!!

© Collaboration Christina Brown and Nita L. Chase 2012

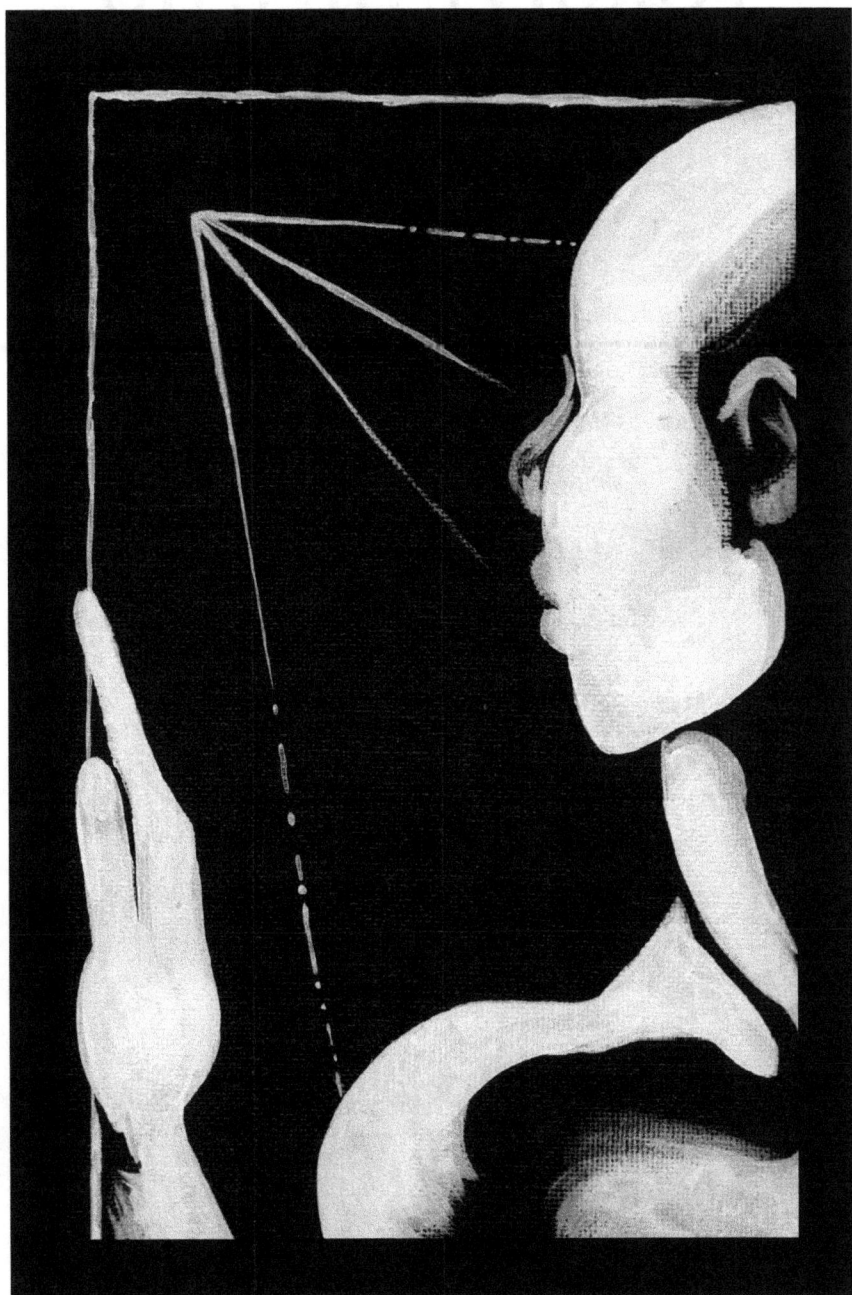

FORGIVE HE WHO NEVER WAS

How

How do you forgive he who never was

Oh he was the donor that harvested my mother's seed

that grew into the me who now is

But he never was

There to photograph my moment by moment highs and lows

There to follow the tracks of my tears

There to stand with me against my foes

There during my nightmares to soothe my fears

How

How do you forgive he who never was

Oh his name was inscribed on my certificate of birth

that gave me the right to wear his surname

But he never was

There to lift me above my reach
There to carry me across the pond
There to design and build my castle on the beach
There to leave his mark and seal our bond

How

How do you forgive he who never was

Yes he was a photograph on the shelf
that reflected some of my facial features

But he never was

There

Where I could touch his heart

There

Where I could see his smile
There

— 61 —

Where I could smell his cologne

There

Where I could hear his praise

There

Where I could taste the essence of his life

There

To tell me I was the best of him

How

How do you forgive he who never was

How

How do you forgive he who never was

HOW

How do you forgive he who never was

The same way God

forgave me

when I was not

HIS

© *Nita L. Chase 2012*

A HEART THAT FORGIVES

It's been a long time coming but I'm here today

With a heart to forgive I'm gonna do it Christ' way

I too have compassion to forgive like Christ

Cause when He forgave me He paid the ultimate price

Made the perfect sacrifice

With his blood, his life, and his breath on pause

I gotta now be down...for His cause

With tears and cheers I got a heart to forgive

To be just like Christ is the reason I live

I too have a heart to get past the offense

I can no longer be dense when Christ was the recompense

For everyone who sinned since

With his blood, his life, and his breath on pause

I gotta now be down...for His cause

So the stuff she did yester-eve and yester-day-light

that made me lose sleep on yester- night

and

His abuse and short fuse

my cries from their lies

The passion of Christ forgave all that stuff

And no one can tell me it wasn't enough

With his blood, his life, and his breath on pause

I gotta now be down... for His cause

A heart that forgives

is what I must be

I can do it by faith

not by that I see

I am a heart that forgives

and lives

With my blood, my life, and my breath on praise

I'll be a heart that forgives for the rest of my days

Copyright Nita L. Chase 2012

THE DISCOVERY

I reached into the depths of my heart

and still discovered your beat

Not your beat as at first glimpse

but your beat that continues to thump

to my myriad of musical styles

I opened the corridor of my brain

and discovered I still thought only of you

Not the seedling initially planted

but the willow tree that yet stands in

the midst of my weeds

I unclenched my hand

and discovered the fingers that I yet hold

Not the agile strong fingers of yester life

but those of today

which still strum my sensitive zones

I looked into your eyes

and discovered a clear picture of hope

Not the one of fantasy land and fairy tales
but the one of the reality
that God gives his adopted children

I heard your voice
and re-discovered your sound

Not the mysterious sound of first epiphany
but the one that heralds and soothes
my season of triumphs and trials

I inhaled
and again, discovered your aroma

Not the one I smelled in passion year one
but the perfume of savoring marital relationship
without becoming a scented divorce decree

I discovered you again

In heart

In thought

In sight

In touch

In sound

In smell

In love with you

I am

Again

© *Nita L. Chase 2012*

I DARE YOU TO COURAGE

I dare you

to love a good man

when a bad man splintered and splattered

your very essence

once upon a time

Can you have that courage

I dare you

to carry the seed

deposited in your temple

by a temple robber

who never was punished

for the crime.... that time

Can you have that courage

I dare you

to resurrect yourself

after falling off the tight rope of life

landing on the outskirts of Death Valley

where the grim reapers of the world

dig your grave

Can you have that courage

Will you have that courage

I had that courage

I have that courage

What about....state your name_____

I dare you!

© Nita L. Chase 2012

MY VISION OF YOUR LOVE AIN'T PERFECT BUT WORTH IT

My vision of your love ain't perfect but worth it

I see a vision of worth

in the awkward unique curl of your smile

that causes ripples and billows

in the heart of my belly

My vision of your love ain't perfect but worth it

I see a vision of worth

in the twinkle in your eye

that tells stories of us

too graphic for their eyes to photograph

My vision of your love ain't perfect but worth it

I see a vision of worth

in the ears that listen

to my silent screams

and interprets my soundless needs

My vision of your love ain't perfect but worth it

I see a vision of worth

in the brain that seeks wisdom

to master the intrusion and confusion

that sometimes live on my highway

My vision of your love ain't perfect but worth it

My 20/20 vision of your love ain't perfect

But

the sum total of you

is worth it

And the perfect God of love

has given us this time

to continue to visualize

until we meet

in perfection

© *Nita L. Chase 2012*

SENIOR MOMENTS

Beyond reason beyond rhyme

for a sixty-second space in time

I need to address seniors right now

for when I reflect on your years, I holla wow

I now remember the moments you gave me sound advice

Back then I was too young and dumb to think about it twice

But as I age towards my senior moments this day

I realize there was and is much truth in what seniors say

I now see the truth in what you said and did

And mama said and papa said will no longer be hid

For I now know there was real wisdom in your heart

And like many I wish I'd accepted it from the start

I should have recognized a seniors' worth years ago

By your examples we live, learn, and grow

For to live to be senior you must have passed the test

So I take this moment to salute you and call you blessed

© *Nita L. Chase 2011*

I WASN'T THINKING, A FEELING FELT

I wasn't thinking I was feeling

Feeling the pressure of peers
Feeling the drip drop of tears
Feeling the pulsing and tingling below
Feeling yes yes instead of no no

I did not think I felt

I felt the power of the touch
and ripples, palpitations, and such
I felt the swelling of my breast
I felt the need for more not less

I wasn't thinking I was feeling

Feeling that time that space
Feeling the chills and thrills in that place
Feeling my heart leap and pound
Feeling that no one else was around

I did not think I felt

I felt sensations from deep inside
and had no desire to end the ride
With each new twist and turn I felt a glow
at that moment I refused to say whoa

I wasn't thinking I was feeling

I did not think I felt

And my non-thinking but all feeling
felt a consequence defined

Baby Boy

© *Nita L. Chase 2013*

A SEASON OF NO INTIMATE ENCOUNTERS

Hearing and feeling our laughter

sharing and carrying our pain

I remember when....

Your laughter walked into my life

and immersed me in sunshine and daisies

uncovering the darkness

coloring the weeds

You shared my rainbows

lifted me out of potholes

I never thought....

Now I am cold

in this winter of frigidity

Who would have imagined

we

would have a season

of

no

intimate

encounters

© *Nita L. Chase 2012*

Chapter 4

YOU DON'T KNOW JACK

It Was Not

Just Give Me the 411 for My 911

Riddle Me This

You Don't Know Jack

The Real Face Book

Lies Have It

Back to the Garden of Eden

Woman to Woman, Generally
Speaking

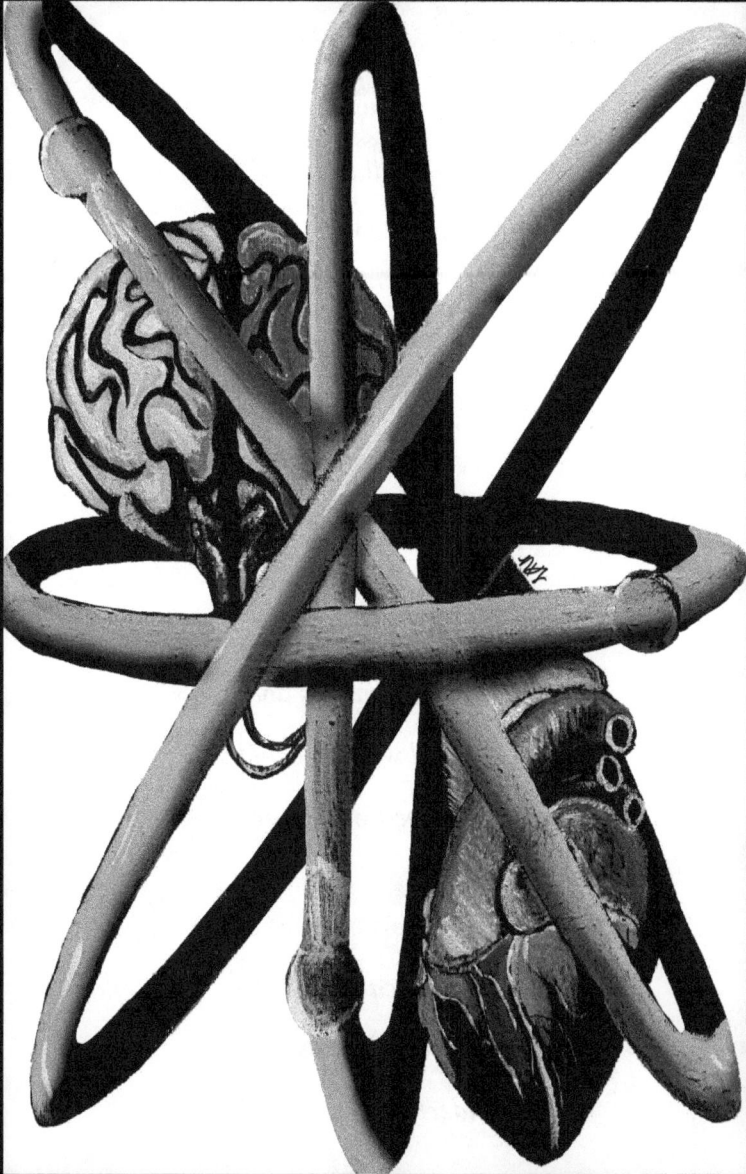

IT WAS NOT

I left my stall

to enter another's gate

and I will tell Y'all

I fell for the wrong bait

It was not cleaner

to graze elsewhere

The grass was not greener

and I did it on a dare

I tried another bed

to check the firmness and size

And after all was done and said

the new bed was no prize

The firmness mutated soft

Then much to my hurt

that bed wasn't used oft

and underneath was much dirt

I thought her shoes cost more

so in them I began to walk

I felt pain I hadn't felt before

saw sights of which I can't talk

They soon lost their shine

and became old and worn

I now regret they're mine

in them I'm lost and forlorn

Transparently speaking

The stall was not cleaner

The grass was not greener

The new bed appeared super sized

But in reality, was no prize

Her shoes weren't designed for me

Only her pain did I see

And

It was not... rapture

It was not... bliss

If you venture

you too take the risk

to discover

It was...Not

© *Nita L. Chase 2013*

JUST GIVE ME THE 411 FOR MY 911

I've got a 911

and all I need is the 411

I don't need you to tell me about

Coulda, Woulda or Shoulda

I don't need you to

sermonize or harmonize

I don't even have a sec

to meet you at the crossroads

or hear your sob story

Just give me the 411

for my 911

I've got a 911

and all I need is the 411

I need the 411

not a recitation

from an inspirational station

I need the 411

before my 911

becomes catastrophic

I need the 411

before I R.I.P.

Just give me the 411

for my 911

Stop hurling questions

that insult my injury

Quit punching that clock

while I tick tock to no return

Cease broadcasting my 911

for you don't have a permit

Just give me the 411

for my 911

I've got a 911

and all I need is the 411

If you don't operate

in the 411

TRANSFER THIS CALL

© Nita L. Chase 2013

RIDDLE ME THIS

Riddle me this

How can my beauty be defined
by the image in the mirror you behold
It only reflects your portrait

Riddle me this

How can the ruler in your hand
measure my stance in the universe
The Ruler of Life is immeasurable

Riddle me this

How can you feel my heat
when you've never been in the fire
of my volcano

Riddle me this

If distance makes the heart grow fonder
why aren't the rich and famous

in love with the poor and lonely

Riddle me this

If life is just a stage
and everyone plays a part
why isn't everyone on the payroll

Riddle me this

Riddle me that

This or that

Still a riddle...

Unanswered

© Nita L. Chase 2012

YOU DON'T KNOW JACK

You don't know jack

You only think you do

Girlll

You don't know my world

Boyyy

You can't fathom my joy

You don't know Jack

You only think you do

And some of what you think ain't true

You don't even have a clue

that sky is only seen blue

and how do you spell roux

You don't know jack

You only think you do

And you don't know Jill

or how I really feel

Lady, you don't know my shoes

Man, you can't feel my blues

You don't know Jack

You only think you do

You don't know my past

why my tick tock goes too fast

You don't know the tears I cried

and how many were because you lied

You don't know jack

You only think you do

You don't know my purse

nor who I had to nurse

You don't know my secret score

or if I once was a whore

You don't know Jack

You only think you do

You don't' know who I sexed

or the witches I vexed

Don't know who gave me DNA

nor the life I lived yesterday

You don't know jack

You only think you do

You don't know what's in my head

or if I sleep when I go to bed

You don't know my battle scars

or the number of my waged wars

You don't know Jack

You only think you do

Don't know if I like it fast or slow

neither what makes me flow and glow

Nor the name of the one who hurt me so

or who's my friend and who's my foe

You don't know jack

You only think you do

So get back

Jack-off ...

and try to know

YOU

© *Nita L. Chase 2013*

THE REAL FACE BOOK

Am I on Facebook

Maybe not the one on which you look
But I find my face
in that special place
with the Alpha and Omega book
chilling by the peaceful brook

Am I on Facebook

Maybe not on your page
so popular in this new age
appears to be all the rage
riding on the latest craze
My face is in the book of praise

Am I on Facebook

Maybe not the one on which you've been
trying to find a new and old friend
My name and face are found
on solid and holy ground

in the book called heaven bound

Am I on Facebook

Maybe not the one that has you on a hook

and sometimes causes you to be a crook

My face I'd rather press

in the book greater than the rest

to find the one who is truly the best

Am I on Facebook

hmmm....

*Are you in **The** Book*

© *Nita L. Chase 2012*

LIES HAVE IT

Lies have

It

Lies

they have

It

The it factor that multiplies

into a daily confession of

I can't

into a daily confession of

I will always be

into a daily confession of

it has always been this way

Lies have

It

Lies

they have

It

The wow factor that mesmerizes one

into the state of
never ending paralysis

into the state of
never ending confusion

into the state of
never ending pessimism

Lies have

It

Lies

they have

It

The ability to transform a dream of success
into a nightmare on your street

The ability to change your freedom status
into a prison without bars

The ability to metamorphosize your Garden of Eden

into a catastrophic valley of death that fright night can't mimic

Lies have it

Lies have

It

But only if you believe

the

It

© *Nita L. Chase 2013*

BACK TO THE GARDEN OF EDEN

Take me back there

There

before the lies

Where

the FBI had no eyes

To

a garden devoid of spies

True

no sighs no cries

Let me return to the easy breezy

before I saw sleazy

or ever met greasy

Bid me return to the days of Adam and Eve

Where work was to only believe

Where all animals lived as one

And man did not carry a gun

Take me back there

There

before tribulation and trial

Where

life was a smile

To

a garden blooming with style

True

oasis-garden of the Nile

Bid me return to the peaceful brook

before I crossed the path of the crook

preceded to gaze at Captain Hook

and learned other monstrosities in a book

Take me back there

There

before drugs and porn

Where

the butterfly kiss was first born

To

gardens glistening in the morn

True

life without scorn

So take me back

there

as in the beginning

© Nita L. Chase 2010

WOMAN TO WOMAN, GENERALLY SPEAKING

Woman to Woman

I don't trust you

It's true

Trust you I never did

and this fact I've never hid

Although God created you grade A best

you failed to pass His trust test

Woman to woman

I don't trust you

Trusting you would be like spelling roux

Most people don't know how to

You were competitive from the start

That's how satan pulled a trick on your heart

Woman to woman

I don't trust you

No way boo boo

For you often change your hue

You play the blame game better than men

And will do almost anything to win

Woman to woman

I don't trust you

You laugh or cry on cue

For a price anyone you may woo

From the beginning you've used sex to trick or treat

And many Samsons have fallen by your feat

Woman to woman

I don't trust you

On this please chew

until You see my point of view

We can be girls as long as we vibe

But trust between us ain't nothing but jive

Woman to woman

I don't trust you

This you knew before I gave you a clue

And quite frankly woman you don't trust me

That's just who we women be

Even though one or two of you I call friend

Trust still becomes an issue when and then

For I know a woman can bake a gourmet lie

But after you dine together tears you may have to cry

Woman to Woman

I don't trust you

and I am sad

The lack of trust between us makes me mad

Will we ever earn each other's trust

and learn to walk together in a state called just

Woman to Woman

I don't trust you

Do you trust me

Generally speaking

See

© Nita L. Chase 2010

YES, I AM MY SISTER'S KEEP-HER

Yes, I am my sister's keep-her

I am the keeper of the prayers
I make often on her behalf

Yes, I am my sister's keep-her

I am the keeper of her weaknesses
that I protect without exposition

Yes, I am my sister's keep-her

I am the keeper of her secrets
that I refuse to breathe into the atmosphere

Yes, I am my sister's keep-her

I am the keeper of our memory lane experiences
that document our historical journey

Yes, I am my sister's keep-her

I am the keeper of the band of love we share

that may be stretched but never broken

Yes, I am my sister's keep-her

I am

my sister's keep-her

And as long as I am

kept by God

I'll keep being

My Sister's Keep-Her

© *Nita L. Chase 2013*

SISTER PLUS

Sister 2 Sister says

blood is thicker than water

But I say

blood clots

sometimes performs disappearing acts

becomes anemic

is prone to infections

often flows in cycles

so give me Sister Plus

Sister 2 Sister says

you are my relative

I ask relative to what

to your tick tock

to your pause in my perfect storm

to affirmations of half-truths

to your weeping willow stance of life

As Einstein stated

relativity is theoretical

So give me Sister Plus

Sister 2 Sister says

you are my next of kin

But I wonder is kin next

when dollars are at issue

when I present a photo opportunity

of your man exposed

when I'm favored to win the game of life

when my beauty fades by the score

and yours by the year

Even the law knows

next of kin is in degrees

So give me Sister Plus

I want

I need

Sister

Plus

Love over law

Faith over fact

Grace over gossip

Mercy over money

Patience over pride

Wisdom over warfare

So Sister

give me

Sister

Plus

© Nita L. Chase 2010

SISTER APOLOGY ACCEPTED

Sister

It did hurt when you stepped on my toe

then acted just like you didn't even know

I used my pain as a time to grow

So apology accepted

And sister

I know you got caught up in the game

and added fuel to the flame

as those others smeared my name

So apology accepted

Yes sister

There was that time on me you lied

and a rain fall of tears I may have cried

But I moved past my anger and pride

So apology accepted

Now sister

Some of my secrets you did not keep
and caused my spirit to moan and weep
But upon you coals I will not heap

So apology accepted

Oh by the way sister

I saw the frown you gave to me
and your beautiful smile I did not see
But I will wait until you find the key

So apology accepted

I accept your apology

Unwritten

Unspoken
Spoken
And let us both now agree

It's more than a mere token

Again, your apology I do accept

After all, for this too my Jesus wept

Yes today I still rise

From my heart I too apologize

For in a state of forgiveness

the peace of God will rest

And sisterly love can forever be

for you my sister and for me

Sister

Apology accepted

© Nita L. Chase 2012

STOP BEING SUSPICIOUS OF SELF

Girl

You need help

You need to stop being suspicious of your self

You see

I'm tired of telling you

that when you entered the room

Only you

thought we were staring

Only you

thought we were glaring

Only you

saw rejection based on the guilt you were carrying

Girl

You are suspicious of your self

I used to be like you but I turned to Jesus for help

The guilt you've been carrying we never knew

And yes about it you may have told few

But we in this place have not a clue

of what you stirred in your stew

Girl

You are suspicious of yourself

I used to be like you, but the Rock hid me in his cleft

No, that Sister did not change seats because you appeared

She was not laughing because she thought you were weird

And into your life we have not peered

We are far too busy getting our own debris cleared

Girl Welp

Stop being suspicious of yourself

You see I can't waste time being suspect

I'd rather detect

every opportunity to erect

that I have no regret

Interject

proclaim and project

Christ

who is above suspicions

Correct!!!

© *Nita L. Chase June 6, 2012*

I STARRED IN "FOR COLOURED GIRLS"

I starred in "For Coloured Girls" first at the age of five

and truly it's a miracle that I am alive

beyond that...still I thrive

For that role was in the devil's den

where innocence was lost in that demonic sin

I was battered and bruised in that role

by that evil leading man who had no soul

I starred in "For Coloured Girls" from a role I could not sord

I never got an award

Neither was I with the cast on the billboard

My home became center stage

and Father Protagonist acted out his rage

Even molestation was on the page

with no consideration for my age

I starred in "For Coloured Girls" without remuneration

but the supporting cast got some compensation

I alone felt condemnation

One of my characters was A Boar Shun

The part was relentless, not a second of fun

The cast applauded my take on the role

But if the truth be told

each act left me cold

I starred in "For Coloured Girls" and they never gave me a dime

The villain's role was prime

He received payment for his time

This villain appeared as a mild-mannered sheep

until he robbed my pasture and made me weep

He mesmerized

burglarized

finally traumatized

To add insult to the intrusion

on my debut of confusion

at finale' it was labeled only an illusion

I starred in "For Coloured Girls" and never got reimbursement

The others were reimbursed for their time spent

and I never got to vent

Frienemy starred as a rapist in one act

He called it fiction, I called it fact

In some movies he's called Mister

in others Twista

Either Mister or Twista

ravished this Sista

I starred in "For Coloured Girls" and never got paid

My co-star's images are just beginning to fade

But today I am starring in a new role

with the Passion of the Christ in my soul

It took a lot praying to get on this present stage

to let go the anger and rage

My spirit is now at peace and not at war

For today

Today

TODAY

In God I am

and God

directs this Star

© *Nita L. Chase May 2012*

JESUS IN THE MIDST OF MY LIFE

Sister I am in the midst of life

trying to stick and stay

With each turn my staying goes array

My sticking slips on slippery slopes

and I can't move

can't breathe

I can only

whisper

Jesus

I keep crying

how long

how far

how low

must I be

to see

only You

I know He answers

but I don't hear

yet

But

I am glad

I can still whisper

Jesus....

Sister

Did you hear me

© *Nita L Chase November 2012*

HUSH SHUSH SISTER

Hush Shush Sister

At this moment God is calling

And if on my knees I be crawling

both my eyes be balling

with every burden I be hauling

not one more moment shall I be a stalling

until I claim that moment with Him

Hush Shush Sister

Hush Shush Sister

At this moment God is talking

Though I don't always do it His way

or always have the right words to say

or often tell temptation nay

I hear God today

Hush Shush Sister

Hush Shush Sister

At this moment God is calling

And if you don't hear His call

or you have the gall to not fear the fall

I won't be locked in your stall

I'd rather be like Paul

Hush Shush Sister

Hush Shush Sister

At this moment God is walking

And though I am learning how not to sin

I hear God's call to be His friend

For Him I now have a strong yen

Because with Him I know I win

Hush Shush Sister

Hush Shush Sister

At this moment God is near

Stop trying to wax up my ear

to try to cause me not to hear

when His call is now clear

From His path I refuse to veer

For I now can answer God's whisper

Hush Shush Sister

© Nita L Chase March 13, 2011

I WAS IN THE VAGINA MONOLOGUES...WITH THEM

Lisa was one of them

Her vagina was strong willed, bold, and wild

never confused with meek and mild

With talent and wit, she played a marvelous Eve

and it wasn't just because she had on the Eve weave

Canethia was one of them

Losing her hair made her talk in a baby voice

For this part she was the perfect choice

She was Proverbs 31, but we glimpsed her crazy side

while she was on the hair-merry-go-round ride

Rose Mary was one of them

She was wisdom, grace, but with gangsta style

Watch out world Rose Mary maybe on the prowl

For now that she's mastered the piece called "Flood"

She's owning her new self...a seed primed to bud

Tina was one of them

She was there in that room

She played her part right next to her daughter's womb

I remember...she took me there on stage

Her performance was more than lines on a page

Ashlee was one of them

She was a reminder that the last shall be first

Cast near the end she quenched my thirst

And not only in the workshop was she down for the cause

She was a backstage hoot and for that I too give applause

Sarah was one of them

She really showed it to us as she did Bob

The audience and I loved her fantastic job

When she did her lap dance in the chair

It brought the house down I do declare

Sabrina was one of them

She played two faces of Eve and touched the heart

And I was in awe of the depth of her part

This play would not have been the same without her there

For she made the audience stop and stare

Monica was one of them

Bryan will never be just another name on a page

Not after the way she said his name on stage

And she was electrifying displaying a device to shock

Quite frankly…. she tick tocks to a divalicious clock

Demaris was one of them

OMG she was a brave choice

She brought it in more than just her voice

On and off stage she went to a crazy state

And her performance spot on…first rate

Sheena was one of them

She was the Coochie Snorcher that did

things backstage that should have been hid

But on stage she shined in her role

Coochie Snorcher was pure gold

Nidga was one of them

When Nidga made a statement in her short skirt

everyone in the audience was on high alert

She was casted last but her performance first rate

And all she could say was "don't hate"

Stephanie was one of them

Her vagina was angry and pissed

She brought it, and did not care who she dissed

But her on stage cum scene and her display of a thong

had many in the audience wanting to sing angry vagina song

Siona was one of them

She released a giant baby in her part

and allowed the audience to see a crack in her heart

But when they saw her legs, they lost focus

Some may have thought OMG or hocus pocus

Nette was one of them

She was our very own VMR extraordinaire

And truly she delighted the atmosphere

She reported on the vagina in truth and fact

Thank God she was a class act

Kathy was one of them

OMG Miss Kathy...Ms Kathy...Mrs. Kathy I now am led

only to say "nuff said"

Tier was one of them

The splendor of her vagina dance did amaze

And some of us were in a daze

Her movements were perfection and bliss

I wanted to give that girl a kiss

Erin was one of them

On the last day of the show

her vagina danced powerfully to let the audience know

all the things the cast did not say in word

and to reiterate in dance the words already heard

Janice was one of them

Her vagina was engaged behind the scenes

Her vagina worked hard in those jeans

To me she was one of the cast

and with us she can now shout "at last"

I was in the Vagina Monologues with them

Oh, I almost forgot him

Lucas, *our vagina loving man*

who was also a stagehand

And he learned more about vaginas than he ever knew

Too bad he's just one of the few

Eric was one of them

Wow!! As Director he chose the perfect cast

He never lost his focus and stayed on task

He directed with understanding and love

He had not a vagina, but God blessed him from above

I was in the Vagina Monologues with self

And I pulled all kinds of moans off the shelf

I gave the audience the pleased vagina sounds

And yes, I moaned several good rounds

I was in the Vagina Monologues with them

And in each one I found a gem

I give my God all the praise

For my spirit He did raise

on the journey with all of them

above the rim

to our own unique fabulous wonder

I'm gonna miss them and their vagina thunder

© *Nita L. Chase April 15, 2012*

ABOUT THE AUTHOR

Nita L. Chase, named, 'Nita Louise' by her beautiful mother, Erma Lee Johnson, is a lover and servant of God first. As a bonus she is wife to Alvin Chase, Sr., mother to three wonderfully intelligent sons; Preston, Alvin Chase, Jr. (AJ), and Desmond. She is also a sister, aunt, cousin, and friend to a large extended family. Born in Indianapolis, Indiana, and raised in the deepest parts of the South, Nita grew up in Clarksdale, Mississippi.

As a child Nita's writing began to take form, however, the message met the carrier far too soon so Nita would often discard her work. It wasn't until later in life did she realize her writing was not only a gift, but intended as a tool to express her intimate relationship with God, man, life and love.

For Nita, poetry is not about how much recognition she obtains, rather it is the artistic utterance of her soul. Through writings such as 'Whisper Epiphany', and now "Passion Speaks", Nita idealizes the context in which the art stains her life. She says,

Poetry is my whisper

breathed through uncensored lips

and oft times my shout

about the other one's eclipse

It's my own dance of words

and rendition of word play

and with each poem exhaled

my soul sings that day

As a poet and orator, Nita has eloquently delivered sassy messages of hope, love, and laughter, with a little bit of spice, through her poetic interpretations for special events, ceremonies, and programs nation-wide. Nita has played an instrumental role in establishing the spoken word culture on the Mississippi Gulf Coast and has started her latest venture as the Transformational Motivational Poet, providing poetry on demand.

When she is not speaking through poetry, by day Nita can be found in courtrooms serving as a lawyer or sitting on the bench as a Family Master Judge. She obtained her Juris Doctor degree from the University of Mississippi, Oxford. She is the co-owner of Chase Chase & Associates, PLLC Law Firm.

For over 20 years Nita has served her church, Victory International Christian Center (VICC) as a key leader. When she's not serving through the VICC, Nita is serving with her illustrious sisters of Delta Sigma Theta Sorority, Incorporated.

In all that she does there is one common thread amongst the chord, passion.

www.ingramcontent.com/pod-product-compliance
Lightning Source LLC
Chambersburg PA
CBHW070045100426
42740CB00013B/2807